BEATRIX

Various Episodes from the Life of Beatrix Potter

JEANETTE WINTER

FRANCES FOSTER BOOKS
FARRAR, STRAUS AND GIROUX
New York

When Beatrix Potter's own words from her published letters and journals are used, the text is set in italics.

Copyright © 2003 by Jeanette Winter
All rights reserved
Distributed in Canada by Douglas & McIntyre Ltd.
Color separations by Hong Kong Scanner Arts
Printed and bound in the United States of America
by Berryville Graphics
The text of this book is set in Cheltenham
The initial caps are from an early-twentieth-century
hand-lettered alphabet by Harry E. Townsend
Designed by Jeanette Winter and Judythe Sieck
First edition, 2003
1 3 5 7 9 10 8 6 4 2

Library of Congress Cataloging-in-Publication Data

Winter, Jeanette.
    Beatrix : various episodes from the life of Beatrix Potter / Jeanette Winter.
        p.   cm.
    Summary: This simple biography of Beatrix Potter, best known for writing The tale of Peter
Rabbit, includes excerpts from her published letters and journals and reveals why she drew and
wrote about animals.
    ISBN 0-374-30655-9
    1. Potter, Beatrix, 1866–1943—Juvenile literature.   2. Authors, English—20th century
—Biography—Juvenile literature.   3. Artists—Great Britain—Biography—Juvenile literature.
4. Children's stories—Authorship—Juvenile literature.   5. Animals in literature—Juvenile
literature.   6. Animals in art—Juvenile literature.   [1. Potter, Beatrix, 1866–1943.   2. Authors,
English.   3. Artists.   4. Women—Biography.   5. Animals in art.   6. Animals in literature.]
I. Title.
PR6031.O72Z6966 2003
823'.912—dc21

[B]

2002069724

A little book for little hands

ONCE UPON A TIME there was a little girl with wavy hair and serious eyes, and her name was Helen Beatrix Potter. I am that little girl.

I [was] born in London because my father was a lawyer there.

I live in a tall brick house and spend my days in the nursery on the third floor.

MOTHER and Father tend to their own affairs, leaving the governess, Miss Hammond, to tend me. She tells me tales about the fairy folk who live in the greenwood, far from the gray city sky.

WHEN I was six years old, my brother, Bertram, was born. Mother and Father still tend to their own affairs, but now Miss Hammond tends Bertram, and I am left to tend myself.

The lonely days have begun. No one has the time for me. I talk to the birds, who have the time.

I talk to the mice in the garden, who have the time.

I was always catching and taming mice.

THE *nursery authorities* are too busy to notice some of the secret friends I bring up to the third floor.

Birds in cages are allowed. Human friends are discouraged. Mother and Father are afraid of germs and bad influences.

I had been discontented and never strong as a young person in London.

Colds and headaches are frequent, especially at Christmastime. Mother and Father take little notice of the holiday, being Unitarians.

Christmas comes but once a year— thank goodness!

EVERY summer the family travels north to the country. Bertram and I roam the grounds of the big rented estates we stay on. Ah, freedom! We watch the wild rabbits play and hide and jump and run, and I tame a few. *I seem able to tame any sort of animal.*

Sometimes at summer's end, Mother and Father allow one of the tame rabbits to return with me to the city.

MY companions lift my spirits. My rabbit, Peter, has learnt to ring a little bell, drum on a tambourine, and jump through a hoop. He is an able student.

NOW and then Father takes time from his affairs to take me to the art museum. Mother still tends to her own affairs.

I soon forget the building. But the pictures burn in my mind. *It is strange how deeply the mind is impressed when excited.*

I do not remember a time when I did not try to invent pictures. I draw Toby and Judy, lizards from the garden. I draw Sally, a ring snake. I draw Punch, a frog. And I draw rabbits wearing clothes.

MY rabbit, Peter, has not learnt to mind his manners while I paint. He finds certain colors good to eat.

HOUSES in the city are populated with house mice, busy behind the walls and under the floors.

I tame one tiny little house mouse and call her Hunca Munca. She is my dear friend and has her own tiny little box to sleep in.

ONE day Hunca Munca climbed to the top of the chandelier in the downstairs parlor. The brass was so slippery that she fell off.

Hunca *managed to stagger up the staircase into [her] little house, but she died in my hand. If I had broken my own neck it would have saved a deal of trouble . . . I do miss her.*

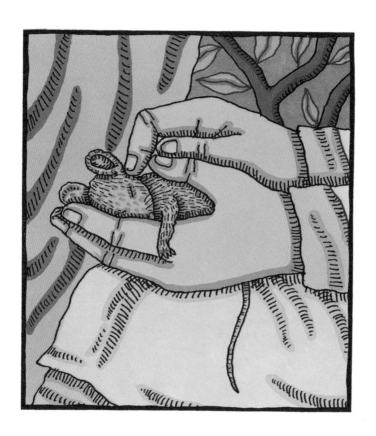

MRS. Tiggy-Winkle, my hedge-hog, is a dear.

She was not a bit prickly with me, she used to lay her prickles flat back to be stroked.

SUMMER trips to the country have become crowded. I can't leave my friends behind in the city. (They travel without tickets.) Mrs. Tiggy-Winkle is always very hungry on a journey.

I walk about in the country twilight by myself, which isn't allowed in the city.

The great harvest-moon rose over the hills, the fairies came out to dance on the smooth turf... and faint in the distance, then nearer and nearer, came the strange wild music of the summer breeze.

I bring my drawings from the country back to the city. They help me imagine I have escaped to the fairy woods.

THE third floor is now my classroom. Bertram has been sent away to school. So I learn alone with my governess, Annie Carter. During the long days I memorize much of William Shakespeare.

I invent my own private secret language to use when I write in my journal. *No one will read this*, I write.

I have stories inside me that I must get out.

A microscope has been added to the schoolroom. I marvel at the magnification of the tiny creatures and am compelled to draw them.

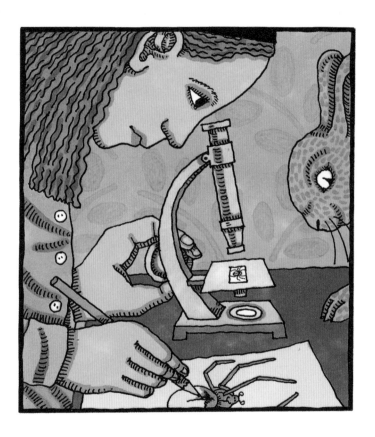

I *cannot rest, I must draw, however poor the result*...whether it be the dead bird I find in the garden, or the beetle crawling in the dirt, or the caterpillar sunning on a leaf, or whatever.

MOTHER and Father have engaged a drawing teacher, Miss Cameron, to guide my efforts. Father is critical of my pictures, and Mother is not interested. Miss Cameron and I have different ideas and cannot come to terms. When she is here I paint as she wishes. *Of course, I shall paint just as I like when not with her.*

I do wish these drawing lessons were over so that I could have some peace and sleep of nights.

AT last the lessons are done. I can draw as I please. I paint as I please, and I photograph my dear friends, the better to draw them. Oh, joy!

I live so much out of the world. Will I ever be connected?

THE third-floor schoolroom has become my studio. I draw and I paint. I look through the microscope. I write in my secret journal, and I write letters to the children of my last governess, Annie.

WHEN her little boy Noel was sick, I wrote and told him a story about a rabbit named Peter.

My dear Noel,

I don't know what to write to you, so I shall tell you a story about four little rabbits whose names were—

Flopsy, Mopsy, Cottontail and Peter.

ONE thing often leads to another. The story letter proved so popular with Annie's children that I made a small little book and called it <u>The Tale of Peter Rabbit</u>.

One little book leads to another little book, and before long I am writing books about all my old companions (and some new ones, too).

I have just made stories to please myself because I never grew up!

*I*T *is something to have a little money.* The little books are quite successful. With my earnings I buy Hill Top Farm, and finally leave the sad gray city behind.

I live here with eighty ewes, forty young sheep, three horses, fourteen cows, lots of calves, twenty-five hens, some pigs, five ducks, a dog, a pony, turkeys, a cat, rabbits, and my dear husband, Mr. Heelis.

It is happily ever after at Hill Top.

AND by the way, from my doorstep I can see ... *a broad space of grass . . . just right for a picnic—or for rabbits to dance on.*

THE END

AUTHOR'S NOTE

BEATRIX POTTER was born on July 28, 1866. She lived at 2 Bolton Gardens, London, until she was forty-seven years old, when she married. Beatrix Potter and her husband lived in a cottage next to her beloved Hill Top Farm, in the Lake District. She died on December 22, 1943.

Beatrix Potter's connection to the world is wide. From the time The Tale of Peter Rabbit *was published in 1902, her books have been and continue to be read by children around the world.*

Her twenty-three little books have been translated into over thirty languages, and millions of copies have been printed and sold.

SELECT BIBLIOGRAPHY

Linder, Enid and Leslie, eds. *The Art of Beatrix Potter.*
   London and New York: Frederick Warne & Co., 1955.
Linder, Leslie. *A History of the Writings of Beatrix Potter.*
   London and New York: Frederick Warne & Co., 1971.
Linder, Leslie, ed. *The Journal of Beatrix Potter.*
   London and New York: Frederick Warne & Co., 1966.
Taylor, Judy. *Beatrix Potter, Artist, Storyteller and Countrywoman.*
   London and New York: Frederick Warne & Co., 1986.
Taylor, Judy, ed. *Beatrix Potter's Letters.*
   London and New York: Frederick Warne & Co., 1989.
————, ed. *Letters to Children from Beatrix Potter.*
   London and New York: Frederick Warne & Co., 1992.